No Sweeter Fat

No Sweeter Fat

poems by
Nancy Pagh

Autumn House Press

PITTSBURGH

ISBN: 978-1-932870-13-8
Library of Congress Control Number: 2006933891

for James Bertolino,
who gives so much to poetry

The Autumn House Poetry Series

Michael Simms, General Editor

• Winner of the annual Autumn House Press Poetry Prize

Acknowledgments

Grateful acknowledgment is made to the editors of the following
publications in which some of this book's poems first appeared:

B.C. Studies: "Bait"
The Bellingham Review: "After I Die"
Crab Creek Review: "Pig"
Grain: "Answer" and "Picture of Erick off Baranof Island, Alaska"
Jeopardy: "She Might Have Been a Cutter"
Poetry Northwest: "Anchoring"
Pontoon 8: "The Fat Lady Sings" and "Ten Reasons Your Prayer Diet
    Won't Work"
Rattle: "Spring Salmon at Night"
Rock Salt Plum Poetry Review: "August"
Room of One's Own: "Cold Spots"
Tattoos on Cedar (the Washington Poets Association 2006 anthology):
    "Among the Vegetarians"

The text of the found poem "Willendorf Venus, Found," excluding the
final stanza, is appropriated for creative use from the website
http://witcombe.sbc.edu/willendorf/willendorfwoman.html.
The Willendorf Venus resides at the Museum of Natural History in
Vienna, and this image of her is widely used on said website and
others. The poet invented the book title *A History of Art* to suggest any
generic compendium of beautiful art through the ages.

The author would like to thank her supportive parents – Sally and
Richard – and sister – Jeri – and the writers and friends who especially
encouraged, inspired, and tolerated: Jim Bertolino, Anita K. Boyle,
Kathy K. Y. Chung, Sharon Damkaer, George Daneri, Kathleen Engman,
Janel Erchinger-Davis, Gabriele Helms, Jacqueline Howse, Beth Janzen,
Iris Jones, Timothy Kelly, Yasuko Kurono, Carmen Malvar, Joel
Martineau, Carlos Martinez, Brenda Miller, Thelma Palmer, Julie
Walchli, Wini Warren, and Jeanne Yeasting. She also wishes to thank
that astonishing and enduring poet, Tim Seibles, for selecting this
manuscript and thereby erasing the misery of having never been picked
for a team-sport "side" in elementary school.

Contents

I have pried through the strata and analyzed to a hair,
And counseled with doctors and calculated close and found
no sweeter fat than sticks to my own bones.

—Walt Whitman, "Song of Myself"

Blackberries

Blackberries

I would like to write you a poem about fat ladies
but you prefer to read of blackberries.

There are eight hundred sixty-four poems about blackberries
published in English; where is the harm
in another?

So let's say that the wildest fat ladies
grow on low runners that snake
unplanted along the driest hillsides
of coastal British Columbia.
The tight knot of their fruit
is smaller than all others, and shaped
like the bud of your own coldest nipple.

I heard a Sixteenth-Century Italian printer
despaired the destruction of cuttlefish
and began making his books with the juice
of fat ladies.

A transplanted Himalayan variety of fat lady
ripens in cow pastures late in the autumn.
It hangs in black clumps
among serrated yellow leaves, tasting
like barbed wire, hatred, and the mineral note
of self abnegation; your tongue thrills
to meet such darkness.

Royalty used to reserve the color of fat ladies
just for itself, but now
the CEOs all favor a striking red tie.
The American president follows suit.

Fat ladies travel many miles
in the gut of a bear
to colonize the bright waste of clearcuts.
I would like to read the diaries
kept on one of these passages.

Have you ever noticed that the biggest fat ladies
are just beyond your reach?

Fat ladies do not taste
like salmonberries. Salmonberries do not taste
of salmon. Fat ladies taste good
when you are standing near the Nooksack River
watching the salmon
or watching the places you wish there were salmon.

Fat ladies permanently stain everything
except your tongue.

An overripe fat lady drops in your palm
with the slightest touch.
If you try to blow off the roadside dust
you will break its tender skin
and miss the holy communion
of eating the roadside dust.

Oh that first day, that first day you notice
the fat ladies have withered and dried on their vines:
a regret more tart
than the small unripe segments
of the first fat lady
you ate that summer.

Again and again the fat ladies push
in to every unclaimed corner of the neighborhoods,
reminding the soft palates of children
there really are things in this world
so sweet and so free.

There are so many fat ladies; where is the harm
in sprinkling one with sugar
to watch the materialization
of Homer's wine-dark sea?

The Fat Lady Sings

with a voice like melting apricots
bubbling in a saucepan
with black cherries, brandy
and cinnamon notes

you were expecting a horned helmet,
a sports analogy, perhaps?

the fat lady sings
the Frito Bandito song
out of nostalgia for her childhood

sings in spite of your hatred
of her ability to be fat
despite your hatred
of fat

instead of crying

to you
and all you can do is laugh
and count the moles on her face

the fat lady sings
she knows all the words to sea-nymph songs
and has set them to new music

lash yourself to your steering wheel
in the McDonald's Drive-Thru
or her sweet voice
will make you weep for your own unmet hunger
and turn the car around

the fat lady sings
as she pleasures herself
the fat lady's songs
are not necessarily about sex
or food, either

5

the fat lady sings to the smallest fingernail
of a moon, or a full moon
or any moon between these
she does not have favorites

the fat lady sings
well enough to be a pop star
if she lost some weight
and covered a song by Christina Aguilera
and lost some weight

the fat lady sings
the most dangerous song
in the park on a red blanket
where everyone can see her

it is a song about loving herself
and might be addictive
to passers by

but we cannot be sure of that
because no one understands the lyrics

the fat lady isn't always singing
what else is she doing?
something that is apparently never over

until she sings again

Fat Lady Reads

A fat lady reads a book
she reads a book all day
and all day
she is not a fat lady

unless she reads a diet book
or Wally Lamb's *She's Come Undone*
and there's a good chance she reads
one of those.

A fat lady reads a book
and enters a world
where there really are no fat people
of consequence

except old Mrs. Manson Mingott
in Edith Wharton's *The Age of Innocence*
whose "immense accretion of flesh
descended on her in middle life
like a flood of lava on a doomed city"

and except the rude person
repeatedly referred to as "the fat man"
(corpulence meant to represent everything
unaware of its own privilege)
in Bharati Mukerjee's "A Wife's Story."

Wealthy matchmaking fat ladies
and chubby men who use more than their half
of an armrest at the theatre
are just useful minor characters;
the fat lady reads
and identifies with the heroine (or hero)
and we all know who they are.
Their pants fit.

The fat lady understands
you cannot expect regular people

to identify with a tubby Ishmael
or believe he could carry that belly
all the way up the *Pequod*'s spars

or relate with the poet Amy Lowell
who the *Heath Anthology of American Literature* says
was an unattractive, overweight woman,
an old maid, a lesbian
soundly rejected by readers
and reviewed as a failure because
she was "cut off
from the prime biological experiences of life
by her tragic physical predicament."

A fat lady writes a book
she writes a book all year   ·
and all year
she's fat
but never writes about that.

She wants to be a serious writer.
What a tragic literary predicament.

The Fat Lady Is Colored

If the fat lady is brown-skinned
and has long straight dark hair
or short curly dark hair
or some other quantity of hair
and is Métis or from the Lummi Reservation
or from any reservation
or small town
or street with the name of a bird in it
or street that is numbered
or named for a European explorer
or Euclid
or any as-yet unnamed street
or dirt road
or if she lives in an apartment up high above an avenue
or has no fixed address
then she is a Squaw.

But if she is slender and young
she might be an Indian Princess
and you can find one of those
frozen on a collector plate, picture postcard
or U.S. dollar coin.

If the fat lady is Asian
then she is an Oriental, no matter what
she weighs.
She is probably good at math, too,
regardless of her height/weight ratio.

If the fat lady is Oriental she
might have been an exotic mail-order bride
when she was a young girl.
She has run away from the Montana husband
who bought her ticket in 2003
in return for full housekeeping services
and a blow job every night after work.
Her fat is a sign of her disobedience.

Beautiful Orientals are all good
delicate girls, obedient to a fault.
Isn't that sad
and Romantic?

If the fat lady is descended from Africans
then she has a huge ass
 – which would be good for pushin'
if the rest of her was thin –
and slaps uppity youngsters all the livelong day.
She's quite a character.
It's funny to listen to her colloquial language
especially if it's in a film
scripted by White men.

If the fat lady is Queen Latifah
then she is proof that fat women are more acceptable
when they are not White women
especially when they are selling cosmetics
to all the women who buy magazines
when they feel fat.

If the fat lady is Oprah
then hey, she ain't fat no more!
Hallelujah! There's hope for us all.

If the fat lady is colored
White
she is studying up on how to get anorexia
by reading a magazine
with Queen Latifah on the cover.

If a colored fat lady walks down the street
and three White men make fucking motions with their hands
and oink
and she goes home
and writes a poem about their racism
what is that?

Is it a more culturally significant poem
and liable to be widely anthologized
with three White racists
or with one racist
one equal-opportunity misogynist
and another fellow secretly attracted to all colors of fat women
because they remind him of his mother's sweet body
but calling out a hatred
to create distance
between other men and his shame?

Fat Woman with Cats

because she has waited all her life to give this tenderness
stored this tenderness she has to give
aches to give her tender
ness to you

who tell her *nothing tastes as good as being thin*
who tell the funny joke *how do you have sex*
with a fat girl? roll her in flour
and look for the wet spot

because you cannot find the spot, the source, the great wide sea
that every living creature simply longs
to wash gently over another
and any cat can:

                                  can you begin to imagine
                    the oceans of sweetness unleashed in this world
                              if every fat woman was allowed to stroke
                                              one human?

Fat Lady's Bath

You will never see the fat lady in her bath,
never know your casual barb
of *pig, cow, hippo, whale*
struck hard and fast, transforming
her – even now, even years later
and all grown up, in her bath.

You will never know the Arctic backdrop
of porcelain, the beached discomfort
of half-submerged flesh
roiling and hunted even now
even now that the hunter has shuffled
along to some other floe.

You will never see the fat woman in her bath
as she sees herself
menstruating, water turning red
with clots of her blood
like that documentary she saw
in high school – the harpooned beluga.

You cannot comprehend the fierce
resistance she makes
with cupped hands pressing
bath water inside herself,
expelling this spout of gore she knows
as another thing that cannot kill her.

Nothing has prepared you for this
wilderness in the fat lady's bath
and you will never be able to swallow
the effluvial hatred that remains
after she rises, clean,
from the draining tub.

Fat Girl Haiku

1.
Stand still on this scale
How'd you go and get so big?
Let's make pie, honey

2.
Third-grade valentines
Every classmate picks for me
The same hippo card

3.
The gay boy likes me
Crouched in the ditch at recess
We're safe together

4.
Dad's arm around me
Have you seen him look so proud?
Just lost twenty pounds!

5.
Don't eat the ice cream
Don't don't don't don't don't don't don't
Have some willpower

6.
Family photos
Cleverly composed to hide
The fattest daughter

7.
Such a pretty face
~ ~ ~ ~ ~ ~ ~
Such a pretty face

She Might Have Been a Cutter

She might have been a cutter, were she born
some years down the line. But as it was
1976, and before girls on talk shows would
demonstrate twenty ways to slice a forearm
and cry *I don't know why, I don't know why*
she simply dreamed.

                    She dreamed
her grandmother's knitting needles,
thick and hollow, makers of all those afghans
and round throw-pillows for the davenport,
burrowing through the thin skin of her fat arm
toward some urgent blue lode
of something.

                    Something
about holding the heavy needle in her
right fist, drilling it into her
left arm, puncturing the surface of some
rind, taut and hairless,
encasing a skein of rolling veins,
was enough.

                    Metaphor is enough,
sometimes; you have to understand. It arrives
in the night, blanket to the cold sleeper
or tool to knit some bloodless relief
even if we still don't know why.

Willendorf Venus, Found

"a woman with a large stomach
        that   overhangs but does not hide   her
pubic area   a roll of fat extends around her
middle   joining with large but rather flat
buttocks   she is not   as Luce Passemard
has pointed out   *steatopygous*   (that is,
possessing protruding buttock)

"thighs are also large and pressed   together
down to the knees   her forearms   however
are thin   her breasts are full and appear   soft
but they are not   sagging and pendulous
nipples not indicated   genital area would appear
deliberately emphasized   made clearly visible
perhaps unnaturally so

"lack of a face   means she is to be regarded
as an anonymous sexual object   rather than
a person   it is her physical body   what it
represents   is important   braided hair seems
clear   although it has been   suggested recently
she is in fact wearing   a fiber-based woven cap

"nor   it seems   was she ever intended   to lie
in a supine position   her most satisfactory
and most satisfying   position   is being held
in the palm   when seen under this   condition
she is utterly   transformed   as a piece of
sculpture   as fingers   are imagined   gripping
her rounded adipose masses   she becomes
a remarkably sensuous   object   her flesh
oolitic limestone   found above the Danube
twenty thousand years old   soft and yielding
to the touch

"if we dismiss all associations with goddesses
and assume   an objective response   she
might be identified   as simply   a stone

16

-age doll for a child   but this strikes us
as unsatisfactory   as she is   a remarkably
realistic representation   of a fat woman
a condition   it has been suggested   due to
eating   and a sedentary life

"the name *Venus* first used   in a tone of mocking
irony   playfully reversing the appellation
Venus pudica   modest Venus   because
the emphatic vulva's labia   the prominent
slightly protruding pubic area   which he tastefully
refers to   and now Venus has become
the collective term   used to identify all obese
statuettes   and pleasantly satisfied   certain
assumptions   at the time   about the primitive
about women   about taste   a rich, male joke
a failed Venus   not beautiful   visibly female
but not feminine   she fails   miserably"

Then again   you might be an eighteen-year-old
fat girl   just like I was   standing in tight
jeans   in the orange-carpeted community college
library   looking through   *A History of Art*
entirely uncomplicated   by matters   of irony
unearthing your own figure   for the first time
in a book of beautiful things   astounded
the world had kept this   secret from you   You
who would be their god   soon enough

Cold Spots

In the club-foot tub I lie
with my breasts
which are everywhere.

Cold, unhappy dumplings
holding themselves back
from the water –
there is too much of them
to submerge with me.

To heat my blood
and send it pounding
through these snowballs,
I add hot – hot –

Hot until my abdomen stains
and fingers swell and redden.

Two limp fists crawl out
and crouch like cooling lobsters
on chilled unpatterned plates.

These breasts don't know babies
or lovers
or sunlight, even:
uneducated boobs
held back since third grade.

Pig

I should marry a pig.
I am not go getter
but I have hidden talents
says the paper place mat
at the Chinese Canadian Food Restaurant.

I could marry a dragon.
I should not marry a mouse.
You are a dragon.
It says here you will be unhappy
if you marry me.
This does not seem right.
Someone should have cross-checked this possibility.

The sweet and sour has that peculiar orange color
of the Chinese Canadian Food Restaurant.
I tell myself such advice should not matter
since I'm not Chinese.
Still, I hate to think an ancient wisdom predicts
I might love you, then make you unhappy.
Worse, I hate to think you may have known this
all along, without the place mat.

With rings from my glass of water
I moisten the place mat corners
tear off bits of paper
roll them into pellets.
I think for a long while.
(My hidden talent is making pellets.
My hidden talent is stacking pellets.)
I decide you really *are* a pig;
this thought makes me feel better.

The menu suggests family combinations
numbers 1, 2, 3, 4, 5.
Pigs, roosters, monkeys – is rabbit the same as cat?
I am a woman comforted by warm orange food

willing to believe anything
even the description of imported beer
offers direction:

"Go well with Chinese food.
Blend in with spicy dishes."

Driving with Greg Chan

it's Vancouver and raining   on 4th Ave
the slick   the gray
the wipers   his warm round face

new friends   tasting   our lives
his brown warm face   new to me
beautiful   dimpled   and

dear, almost   round brown face
I'll say it: different
than every white man I've known

different lips   mouthing   this
difference   of being   Greg Chan
hyphenated   Canadian   always

brown   but what he wants
to know   is   do I think of myself always
as a white girl   do I see race

perpetually   like he must?   I see
runny stoplights   over   my winter
hands on the steering wheel

suddenly   plain   normal   hands
No   I say   *No*   is the half-truth
I offer Greg Chan   while the blades

switch   across the windshield
and the moment to say   I think of myself
as a fat girl   passes

unspeakable   even though   his warm
brown eyes   might have been the first
man's to see   this weight   and understand

or might have said   it's not the same
not the same   not the same thing   at all
you could change   if you really wanted to

light goes green   and we move
through the intersection   under curtains
of rain making   this terrain invisible

G.B.S.

if you think I meant the *global positioning system*
you have wandered into the wrong poem
and got lost
in a dark wood
with wolves and witches
and hungry children
who satisfy themselves by eating candy
then die in an old lady's oven

this is the forest
of Snow-White and Rose-Red
the good daughters
who let the bear in from the storm
and brush the snow from his fur
and stroke his head so prettily
he growls by the fire
in pleasure

this is the forest
where one good turn
causes the girls to meet with the bear
under different circumstances
and not get eaten

instead
a kindly woodsman
uses his sharp axe
to vivisect that bear
and reveal a golden-haired prince
who steps out to marry
the prettiest girl

or sometimes, of its own accord,
the bear's skin falls away
in great folds
arranged at the Prince's feet
like a warm brown lake

I personally always imagined
a zipper
the prince could employ
from inside that giant body

I am thinking of that now
as I stand beside my sister
helping her remove her nightgown
so she can take her first shower
after gastric bypass surgery

I think about the woodcutter's axe
when I see for the first time
the ragged line of incision
beneath a trail of surgical staples
running from her sternum
and into her pubis' forest

the surgeon told us
her red and yellow organs
were unusually petite
and she can expect to become
no more than a size six

she weighs three hundred sixty pounds
has a stomach
the size of a walnut now
and is willing to die
for someone golden and lovely
to step out

I lay the nightgown on her bed
and we pad
pad slowly to the bathroom:
two bears
two good bears lost in the woods
on different paths now

Falling

It fell in her thirties.

Her fat fell in her thirties
but didn't go away, not really,
just shifted subtly one day
redistributed itself without quake
without ash just
repositioned itself down
stream, carried below her
bones and ridges
lower down, underneath
the places it had sat atop
before.

Her fat fell one summer
afternoon in her thirties
as she walked to the mailbox
in shorts and observed
her thighs now had a rhythm
all their own a
sort of seismic back beat
to her purposeful stride
and gelatinous, too.

Her fat fell along the gravel
driveway and caused
her to look in the mirror
upon returning to the house
and make the abrupt
acquaintance of her new jowls,
the flap beneath each arm.

It seemed as if her fat continued
falling over the edge of her bed
as she sat there and dressed
each morning
all that long week.

When her fat settled
she had time to survey
the erosion and damned
if she didn't miss the former
full peaks of her breasts so fervently
hidden by sweatshirts. She grew
nostalgic for that solid ledge of belly,
the supple timbers her forearms
were, even the broad landscape
that had been her own face.

Her fat fell in her thirties
causing her to become
sentimental and notice
for the first time ever
that it had all been so beautiful
in the first place.

Ten Reasons Your Prayer Diet Won't Work

1.
Praying to god that you will be thin
instead of eating
only burns eleven calories
at average fervency.

2.
Jesus had large love handles.
I know in the pictures he is skinny
and White
with slightly Italian-esque features,
but he understood the value
of keeping on a few extra pounds
to tide him over in the desert.
If you are a child of god
this runs in your family.

3.
All food miracles create *more:*
more loaves, more fishes, more wine, more manna....
When you ask god to do something about fat
expect multiplication.

4.
The only time you used to talk to god
was giving thanks before high-caloric meals.
Your fat cells remember this
and begin to swell
even at the mention of his name.

5.
God has stock in Doritos.

6.
Eventually you will tell yourself
that god created you this way
and who are you to disagree?

7.
Contrary to popular belief,
eating is not a mortal sin *per se*
and god believes in free will.

8.
Bread and wine. Communion would suggest
god endorses the Mediterranean Diet
instead.

9.
Blasphemy, to waste German chocolate cake.

10.
God is characterized by excess;
your only proof that god exists
is that the natural world is more than it has to be.

Perhaps the closest you've come
to acting in her perfect image
was building your sacred hips.

A Gold's Gym in Bellingham, Washington

What thoughts I had of you on Thursday.
From the elevated cardio deck, perpetually stepping to the edge
of one thought then another, pleasant monotony
of the treadmill's low howl – I saw the two gentlemen,
one gray beard, two gray heads, both tender and old.
While I ambled along on this cyclical highway,
ambled along in my fat-lady sweatpants,
ambled along at my slow-rolling gait, I spied them.

Surrounded by dozens of lifters, each following
his own timeless pattern of repetition and jerk,
these two, a pair, in their loose shorts and patina'd tattoos.
Two kind-faced retirees in knee socks and faded
U.S. Navy tank tops, each counting the other, encouraging,
patient, and waiting his turn at the muscle machine.
So like you, Walt and Allen, that I could see you both here
at the Gold's Gym in Bellingham, Washington.

Here the Asian girl defies every demure stereotype with her back
and the young men do their best to uphold their own –
here America flexes itself beside catalogs of muscles
hung from the walls, and in no universe are the balls bigger
than these flexibility orbits for stretching your spine. Everyone's
here, the housewife, the student, my grocer and me,
some of us watching George Bush's latest war on t.v.,
and all of us fighting too much of ourselves.

I saw you here, Walt Whitman, loafing on the abdominizer bench
while Allen tried every new concoction at the juice bar.
You spotted each other and walked together through the suburbs
of free weights, puzzling over the MP3 players, arguing
the easy philosophy of ubiquitous Life is Good™ t-shirts,
and democratically approving spandex for all. I saw you
grinning codgers sometimes add an unseen finger of weight
to elicit a rivulet of sweat from a beauty – then high five each other.

You shook your heavy head and that straw hat of yours
at the images on the bank of television screens,

and Allen's glasses didn't hide his tears when he came out
from the men's locker room alone. But despite your sorrow,
or perhaps because of it, you clasped your speckled hands together
and headed toward the exit (leading only to car lots and strip malls).
You threw me a wink of encouragement over your shoulder
and I walked on, knowing I'll look for you both in the sauna.

Coming In

Coming In

Because I am a forty-two-year-old woman
and still a virgin,
my mother has decided I am a lesbian
and regularly drops hints to me that it's okay
to come out to her. And sometimes
I have thought perhaps
she's right: after all, she is my own mother
whose understanding of desire built me,
who watched me hold myself
apart from all the other children
and grow these big shoulders
and go through a flannel-shirt wearing phase
and insist I be taken to the doctor
because there must be something wrong with having
these breasts. Sometimes
I would like to come in to my mother.
I would like to hold her once-beautiful hands
and look into her eyes, which are the only eyes left
in this world the same color as mine,
and I would like to tell her I understood
exactly what she meant when she moaned
my father's name over and over in bed at night
even when I was six years old
and slept with my hands tucked between my legs
and she would get out of bed to use the toilet
or have a drink of water
and would come sit on the bed next to me
and stroke the hair from my forehead
and pull my arms from under the covers
and smell my fingers
and make me get up and wash my hands with soap
because I had a dirty habit that would go away
one day, when I found the right man to marry me.
Sometimes I would like to tell my mother
that a very fine imagination ought to buy me
an honorary membership, at least,
into the set of heterosexuality. But then

I say nothing and slip back into a way of being
that has allowed me to remain just as I am:
I look at this world like a skeptical reader
of Old English romances – with knights
and duties and those incredible creatures,
half eagle, half lion. I try to picture one body,
half man, half woman, and frankly
I don't even believe that happens.

Wharf Rats

They have their own knives,
replace their own hooks;
the boys of the locals are serious.
They cast and swear through hot afternoons
on the government wharf at Ladysmith,
ignoring the bees at the bait.

Clam meat has dried like snot to brown legs,
and fish scales cling to their arms.
Their hair is long –
longer than any boy's I know and
redgold yellowgold browngold blackgold.
Each one holds a cigarette in his lips
at a different angle.

My father calls them wharf rats,
and when I ask why they kill the fish
he has to tell me some people eat them.
Vacationing on the white cabin cruiser,
my sister and I catch and release.

Touching only the hook or the ledge of a lip
we shake off each greenyellow perch
while the wharf rats ignore us and smoke.
But how would they feel,
the barbed golden bodies,
pressed to a girl's narrow palm?

Anchoring

With my hands touching you,
a memory of my father
crouched on the bow, on his toes,
the soles of his sneakers toward us –
lowering flat gray anchor and chain,
hand over hand, twenty feet of it,
then soft quiet rope.
He waves one hand to me, the eldest,
to say *put her in reverse*.
Chain draws out across the sea floor
as we drag for a catch.
He motions *stop*, cleats the line.
This subtle, elongated instant I wait for –
a rope drawn to its limit –
the perceptible springing back,

                              anchored.

Watching others anchor and fail: the charterers
who stand on the deck and throw their anchors,
a twirling mass of metal and chain.
The people with money, boat shoes,
black hats with gold braid,
drinking all day from nautical cups
with red and blue anchors.
My father sits, saying *Look at that would you
just look at that* and assures us all
judgment comes to those unfamiliar with "scope."
And that night, or another, it does –
an easterly wind at three a.m.
drags them off to hell.
Or at least, in the morning, they're gone.

That was long ago, only faintly connected
to your sand-brown body –
these patches of hair like coiled gold weeds,
ridges and rib bones are half-buried stone.
My hand travels slowly

charting useless planes,
a soft stretch of belly where nothing can catch.
The ledge of a forearm,
the hinge near your groin
are places to settle in for the night.

I hold you at arm's length a moment,
an elongated instant –
me drawn to my limit –
then perceptibly spring back,

                                   anchored.

Answer

When he didn't answer she heard a family in the distance
in the fog across the beach.
Voices smooth out through a fog and thin themselves
like arrows for long feathered journeys.
Two soft rocks gently tapped
will sound quiet but clear in a fog.

He still did not answer and
that family clambered away, the children's
voices carried on by fog, articulating
barnacle, glaucous, anemone
then white quiet.

She knew she could fill up the silence and
it was hard not to.
She had filled it before.
She was good at it.
She hoped he wouldn't depend on that.

When he spoke he said less than stones, which
say *yes* when you tap them.
He changed the subject
and it evaporated slowly
               or was breathed in
                         or swallowed
                                   like fog across the beach.

Seal

I dream a seal harbored in my salty womb.
Blind, it noses into me like a small fish
in a plastic bucket.

Hands to my drum belly,
I feel its small pressings, small bubbles
rising to a surface

and I become an environment
the islands, reefs, and rocks, the dark green ebb,
the eel grass of Inland Sea.

Not like my girl dreams
(*Pregnant! Who is the father?*)
I know this is all mine.

The lover who went away
the abandonings, real or imagined,
do not matter here.

A flippered member glides
through me
with whiskered curiosity.

Born, she can open the back door
with a nose, manage the steps,
cross the road by herself,

then slip into the dark lake.
Sometimes she comes home after
I am asleep, swimming

toward me under covers
till she settles, soft and black
and slightly wet against my breasts.

Every night
every night
I want this dream.

December I walk the beach at York
and see a thing, a seal, frozen in the tide line.
It's a small one, like in my dreams

but redpurple with black peeling skin –
its head still perfect except the eyes
except the strange white whiskers.

Suddenly public, this debris
demands decision –
am I sleeping or awake?

And I can't believe I'm standing
on a beach so far from home,
in Maine, in my glittering pink scarf

believing dead animals
mean something.

I never have the dreams again.
I never tell anyone.

I seal this story inside myself
and it nudges me
in other ways.

Hysteroscopy

I pray he will find nothing
in that place
while I sleep heavily on the table.
No drawings of buffalo
or lesions left by the spears
that chased them.

I used to ask my little sister,
Did you see the message I wrote
for you on the wall
of Mama's belly?

When I was eighteen years old
I knew the dentist
could read the story
of my first tongue kiss
in the x-rays of my wisdom teeth
before pulling them.

No code the doctor can break,
please. It is enough
that he will pry me open
like a shellfish,
flexing the rigid muscle of me
with a gloved hand,
peering through his hysteroscope
at the articulated brilliance
that comes
after pulling away
the abalone's meat.

Titles of Twenty-Nine Poems I Did Not Write

Winter Moon, Bellingham Bay
Why I Rise at Five a.m.
Tug at Night
Bladder Wrack
Reading Tide Charts
Pain and Slack
Heron, Swinomish Slough
Poem about My Uterus
Sharp Things Found on a Beach
The Male Gynecologist
Why I Would Even Go To a Male Gynecologist
Hike to the Bat Caves, Chuckanut Mountain
Spelunking: A Ghazal
Claustrophobia
The Little Breathing Bats
Droppings
dropping
what he said
seven centimeters
fibroid (a found poem)
Pool in the Woods, Georgia O'Keeffe (1922)
Pelvis Series, Georgia O'Keeffe (1947)
hysterectomy
loss of blood
thirteen ways of looking at virginity
#26
untitled
untitled
untitled

August

By the end of summer
I can walk up the steepest hill
in the neighborhood –
the one cars have to shift down on,
the one you plan your life around
when it snows. I do this
by singing
This old man, he played one
he played knick-knack on my drum
with a knick-knack patty whack
give a dog a bone,
this old man came rolling home
with a slow step for every syllable.
I rhyme one with drum
(we all do)
then two with shoe
three knee
four door
five hive
six sticks, and
then I let him play knick-knack on heaven
(even though that doesn't make any kind of sense)
because I am simultaneously managing
to breathe and walk up this monstrous hill
and maybe the old man is knocking on heaven's door
or maybe heaven is surrounded by a translucent membrane
and he can thrum it like a timpani – a set of them:
different heavens for the various religious sects –
and meanwhile I am conscious of the expansion
of my lungs and the bright gash
of the set sun behind me as I pace
slowly over the crest of this hill
and become newly aware of how much more
my hip sockets seem to hurt when I walk
on the flat and how nice the little breezes feel
on the back of my sweaty neck.
I think there must be a halo of heat

radiating from the top of my head
and into the cooling August dusk,
and because I am the kind of person
who would actually turn to see her own halo
I see the cloud of mosquitoes strung above and behind
my head like a horror-show hairdo of bloodsuckers
and before I can begin to run, in fact
while my mind is debating whether I *could run*
after walking up the Alabama Street Hill,
I feel the small flutter
of an almost poem
just beside my hairline
and suddenly
I am writing a poem
about how this little black bat
is an angel.

Come to the Lake

No, you won't come to the lake, won't step into
your bathing suit or any pool of water
out there, in the world, where people can see

your middle-aged man's body that's been spread
across this continent, a lost marriage, teenaged sons
and somewhere around twenty-two cats.

You tell me you have body consciousness issues.
You've put on a few. You're preoccupied and failing
to see I have body consciousness issues too:

I am conscious of your body every waking moment.
The thought of touching your long brown fingers alone
accounts for half my day. Suddenly I understand

why nothing ever gets done in this world.
All this time, people have been thinking of fucking
one another this way, while I was earning my degree

in virginity. I'm telling you I can lie in bed all day
spinning your story to my uterus and listening
to sounds I've never made before.

I lost a day's work from noticing your brown eyes
are blue rimmed and animated by genetic memories
Caribbean, African, Spanish. I understand

that if you kissed the nipple of my pretty left breast
I would travel someplace there is no road back from;
and if you kissed the nipple of my ugly right breast

I would let you. I know you're tired;
making love to ten thousand women in the Seventies
really wore you out. But come to the lake anyway.

I'll hold both your hands and walk backward.
And when the cool water reaches your genitals
and catches your breath you'll begin to remember

how it was to feel tentative and innocent so long ago
in your own life, when you wanted someone
you thought you'd never have.

Come with me to the lake. I will touch two fingers
to your forehead and baptize you born again
into your own body's sensuality and grace

and again and again into mine.

Sex with the Neighbor

Some times now, as I button my coat
against the damp September morning
and step quietly down the concrete stairs

I imagine my neighbor from the next building
on the third-floor veranda above me
watching me leave for work.

He is the tall Puerto Rican tenant in unit 311,
whose silver bracelets gleam from his arms.
Those loud boys on weekends are his.

A kind and ordinary man in the daylight,
adopter of stray cats, recycler of plastic and glass,
so I don't know why in the early mornings

I imagine him smoking a Marlboro, balancing
his coffee cup on the metal rail and leaning
his whole weight on one arm as languid men will.

He wears a dark blue short-sleeved bathrobe,
which is okay, because it's really still
night out here. And we don't say anything.

All around us the neighbors are dreaming
in their warm beds and even the birds,
even the birds know better

than to make a sound. We don't say anything
or raise our hands to wave
or pass any message at all except that it feels

like sex in a quiet place; you mustn't cry out
to recognize something in each other
across a slowly lightening day.

These mornings I unlock my car and fold up my legs
and imagine the sex with my neighbor
who is only chasing cats in his sleep

only rolling over now to pet the alarm clock,
not lying in bed behind me, my teeth
around his wrist from not crying out.

Anticipation

When that day comes, that afternoon we drive to the ferry
and stay in your car on the car deck, kissing

and missing the view of cormorants fishing, the slick
wet heads of seals – not even noticing passengers

rubbing their bodies at our vehicle's doors
as they squeeze through the line of carefully parked cars

for their coffee; when that day comes and we finally
find our room with its opening windows, opening

sheets, our opening unfolding unguarded hearts;
when that day comes, I will not for one moment forget

the man you are now, your beard like coarse sand
as you tickle my breasts, your hardness and rock

walls and darkest intents. But, when that day comes
I am also looking forward to loving the women

you wear in your arm's silver bracelets, the women
alive in the taste of your skin. I want to meet

that first lover, that schoolteacher who had you,
a sixteen-year-old boy. I want my tongue to examine

the furniture in her New York apartment, exchange
lesson plans, and touch her understanding of desire.

Lori will be there, still nineteen and incandescent,
tucked in that small small fold where you still believe

yes you still believe the alternative to living
is utterly impossible. I want to hold the waste of her life

between my fingers, kiss her like my own daughter
I never had, and never will have. I am going to find

that professor's wife you chased across the country
and so many long-haired voluptuous women curled

now between your toes and even your wife
will not reject my hand as it floats across the surface

of your body in search of the source of so much
goodness and leading, eventually, to this.

Rain

Now that fall has turned this year over
and the rains wake me up at night instead

of summer dreams about your fingers
tracing letters on my sweaty throat,

I lie in my own bed now and listen
toward the smallest perceptible differences

between the sounds of water falling
on the leaves, on the roof, and still

hanging in the sky. And I find
I can still read this rain after all

that never happened between us;
yes the rain is as it always was

and it only makes me happy to know
you are in your own bed next door

awake and really hearing this too
or asleep while my nerves stand

in little rows of attention and listening
enough for us both. Falling in love

is a choice we each make for ourselves;
it is not one of those moments

that just happen to overtake us,
against our will, as we sink to the floor.

Listen to the rain: it comes on like me
and off like you and who can say

the rain doesn't choose when to fall
on its knees all along the pavement?

Gray

I wanted him to kiss me then
        wanted to be quiet
a kind of slack, a calm
        surface flat

all the world's water here
        tugged close
to the moon as possible;
        a high tide. In.

Easing over rock, over
        lichen, the whiskered
roots of trees, to the brim
        of something, some

basin full of some
        settlement, ending even
the salty push
        of winter wind

the slate the stone
        the monochrome
way, the pervasive graying –
        remember the sun?

That was then when I wanted
        him to kiss me loud
a sun in the sky, this being
        a kind of shining

before today:
        this abeyance
everything still like fishes
        suspended and deep

in the rain we all grow gills
            red slashes at our throats
and we open them
            at one another

we pant in our necks
            soft little breathing motions
but this awful still-ness
            of nobody kissing.

What silence
            the withdrawing sea
pretends to uncover – really
            just another noise caught

fish bone deep in the throat
            crosswise and delicate
so transparent, our fragile need
            so unreachable.

Timothy Treadwell

Now I think I could be eaten.
I could be Timothy Treadwell
who loved the bears, loved
the chocolate fur
the lowing, lowing throat sounds
from some place deeper than human
from some other side we never quite get to
in these tender bodies, needful minds.

I could not survive thirteen summers
or spend one night among the scrub alder
where the bears push invisible trails
toward me.

I could not make myself believe
I am bigger, more powerful than a grizzly
so that the grizzly believes it too
and shakes his head from side to side
and ambles slowly, the ground trembling,
away, until the final time, the final bear
does not believe.

But I could let someone I love devour me –
I know this tonight; I know it.
His jaws could tear my scalp away
then settle tight around my throat
to decapitate and push my head aside
and all the while I would be moaning
with my useless human voice
moaning *I love you, I love you,*
you old bear, you beautiful bear,
you beautiful wonderful bear
until I was separate from this body
and this body cloyed inside the bear
and became the thing I loved.

I thought love was good
and maybe it is sometimes for two people.
But the rain falls in straight lines.
People do not want me.
Winter is coming on, coming on,
and alder all around.

Drift

There's a dead squirrel in my neighbor's pond
one ear above the water, green
leaf across its face
and back legs splayed as if mid jump
between the cottonwood trees
reflected in the surface. It drifts
counterclockwise and slow
as a constellation in a summer night:
The Squirrel – another figure to imagine in murk
perhaps with its own chart, like Ursa,
like Canis Minor, Orion's lesser dog – formed
by connecting lines between bright stars
of cottonwood fluff on the pond.

It is slow-motion snowing, puffs of cottonwood
transfixed and lazy in currents of air
and the swallows jet through them,
take and drop and take again –
they must be playing, I think, flashing
white bellies as they ascend and drift
into memories of walking to school,
tin lunch pail, the hill, barn swallows
so agile, so show off, belittling us with speed.
And the underbelly of pier, rowing under
the swallows' nests, mudformed and tucked
to beams above high water's mark – the little clutch
of eggs I stood in the dingy to see.

And I have walked a long way from the pond now
but I drift and drift to the pieces of wood
washed up on beaches, how my father carried them home,
carefully split them with his hatchet in the garage –
the fires all winter
the smell of the cedar, smell of garage,
damp sputter of alder coaxed by the kindling
and being naked with my sister after bathing, naked
and wet in front of a fire, unacquainted with shame,
then the cold hall to white sheets and sleep.

And though I chose not to mention it
I have been thinking of your body all this time,
how it drifts from woman to woman,
is taken and dropped, taken and dropped,
how you float without intention
the way a mind goes when it walks
alone, uninterrupted by love or anyone
coming down the road.

He Must Have Died Young

He must have died young, driving
his father's tractor along the culvert,
along sweet timothy grass and distracted
by the graceful implacability of that hawk
as the little birds chased and raged headlong.
Or from ice on the rigging, coating and coating
the cables and crab cages, laying heavier
through a black Bering night, cold enough
to freeze salt water blown through the air,
until the boat staggered and dropped him,
just a high-school kid, into silence.
He might have been drinking one night.
That would do it. Or the city machines
caught into his finger and pulled
him to violence, addiction, a ripping
despair, a fall from some high building.

One of my girlfriends believes the right man
is born for each of us, is waiting
for the appropriate moment to arrive in our lives.
But I think he died young. These men
I've known are so beautiful, so beautiful
with square-tipped fingers and perfect whorls
pressing perfect marks into me
until I ask if they could love a little
and find they died the worse death –
the same death each.

Maybe I'm wrong and he's out there.
Maybe I'll recognize him by his scars
on the outside: the eye-patched and one-armed man
who escaped the escapable lesser death
to come to me.

Rounding the Point

Walking the shore trail today
I rounded the point and saw
eight pairs of seals in the bay,
dark wet heads bulbous and nodding
together. I saw the current move
across their thick backs and
slight upwellings shadow their turns.
It is November and last year's pups
are heavy as their mothers now,
or perhaps pairs are reuniting
in the gray monochrome bay.

The maple leaves across the trail
unstitched themselves from stem and form,
relinquished all desire.
Look. There were no seals,
but sixteen bull kelp in the bay.
Each bulb was separate as my head,
empty floats in coiling tide.
Why did I want it otherwise?

After I Die

My grandmother's pear or Italian plum
would be comfortable and sweet
but too domestic. I need
a wild tree. Cedar is my favorite trunk
but close-branched;
in cedar I can't see the sky.
Dreamy blossomed dogwood
are too slender for this purpose.
Douglas fir are tall enough and warm
in winter, but I have never felt at home
in a fir. After I die
take me to a madrona.

Choose one red-boled, round-hipped
and open at the shoulders.
Wear pants good for climbing and
bring a few lengths of cord.
Help each other help me
up through the branches,
through rubbery leaves or dry ones,
and tie me supine toward the sky:
I don't want to fall in the first wind.
There are laws against this sort of thing
so choose a place far enough out
that you can't find it again.

After I die the softest places
will come unstitched
and even bitter secrets I kept in my belly
will sound raucous
in the mouths of crows.
Curling red bark of madrona
pulls back from the limbs each summer
and I'll peel too, unwinding from bone.
In rainstorms, hard white pieces,
knuckles and ribs, will drop from branches
through wet green salal. The best part
is being allowed to scatter.

Unaccountable

Among the Vegetarians
(apologies to WW)

Sometimes I would like to turn and live
among the vegetarians –
they are so placid, and so self contained.

They understand the eggplant's secret
firmness, the *tabula rasa* the bean curd is.

I contemplate them long and long.
Death does not linger on their breath.
The darker crevices
of their cutting boards are safe.

They exist without asking another
animal to kneel and spill itself.

The gentle eyes of the vegetarian
flash liquid revelations
to me and I accept them.

Theirs is an appetite to know and be filled
with the scallop the coho the razor
clam's dignity apart.

My hunger takes
the cream-white flesh of the halibut
the migrating eye of the halibut
the scythe-mouthed strike of the halibut
the graveled bed of the halibut
the cold gray sea of the halibut
in every bite.

It is incised, protean, unassuaged
by toast.

My hunger wants more than the halibut
and finds it in the halibut.

Believe me sometimes
I think if you were as much of this world
as the halibut
I would have to eat you too.

Spring Salmon at Night

I thought the west wind called me from bed
the night the river ran so hard.
I followed it over the moonlit lawn
across the road and into the woods,
climbing fallen cedars and moving
beyond the skunk cabbages. I followed
the west wind to the river bed and
plunged my legs in dark water
that sucked and swirled behind my knees
and tried to pull me beyond the bank.

And the wind stopped.
And I forgot why I came out in the night.
And I clenched the underwater moss with my toes
and was lost
until the spring salmon came,
their torpedo-shaped bodies knowing me
as another follower of currents.
In the cold gray river the spring salmon
found and circled me, their forms almost warm
as they touched the backs of my legs
guiding me back through the forest
across suburban lawns and down my own hallway
from bedroom to kitchen
until I found myself standing at the cat-food cupboard
and recognized each cat circling my legs
and my own gullibility
or desire to be led
in the direction of someone else's hunger.

Imaginary Home

When I was twelve years old
I imagined I would live on my own island
in a cabin made of weather-bleached planks
beside a stand of broad-leafed maples.

I wouldn't have a job in the cannery
or picking strawberries on my knees.

The tide would boil in the channel,
and I could hear it at night
from my bedroom, thrumming
slick fronds of the kelp's amber hair.

I would dig butter clams all morning
and eat them in the afternoon.

At the end of day, someone
might pull his boat to safety at my dock
and keep me company. But on an island
I could always see him coming.

Now I am forty in this apartment;
I've tasted no clam in twenty-five years.

It is perfectly clear how
we make our lives islands,
carefully removing the dock for winter
or losing it anyway in a freak summer storm.

There is nothing original
in a metaphor like that.

All I want to know is whether
the poems are the planks
or the fruit of the maples –
samaras, propellers, drifting in air.

The tide is too obvious,
and my mother's the kelp.

Picture of Erick off Baranof Island, Alaska

This one I took when halibut season closed.
Thirty-four hours straight, little brother,
and we saw fluked brown diamonds
every time we closed our eyes
for a week.
Pacific halibut, Greenland turbot, yellowfin sole –
flat panting monsters all over the deck.
Well you were too tired to smile,
too tired to sit.
You stood against that rail, smoking all the way in
to Sitka,
straight like a totem.
This photo remembers dark ruffled water,
white coastal mountains,
uneasy pink sky.
You leaning into it in tall boots, blue jeans,
your torn Norwegian sweater
with nothing underneath.

Show this one to your college friends.
Show them where you go when they ski.
Tell them what this gear can do
to an eye or an arm.
Show them how we're cut, little brother.
Straight
as a diamond
as the halibut.

Bait

My girlfriends take me out for my birthday
to a fish restaurant downtown
and we sit among the crowded plants,
drinking wine, reading menus shaped like fish.
This place is too expensive.
I hold the menu by its caudal fin, lightly,
and choose the cheapest entree: bait.

When I was a girl we stomped on mussels,
cracking their shells to the wharf,
wrapping the warm brown guts around hooks.
They were bait for perch
which were bait for cod.
I remember the wet blue crunch under heel,
the story I told my sister:
This little purple fist inside,
it's the mussel's heart – fish like it best.
After a while I believed the story,
bent quickly to broken mussels
hoping to find a heart, beating.

My entree arrives in a bowl with a lid,
a sort of tackle-box with broth,
and I am afraid of it.
Large ridged mussel shells gape,
their protruding orange bodies seem full
of anatomy. They have beards,
tufts of brown hair there,
near that small purple heart
which is alarming, clitoral,
half exposed between the mussel lips
opened with steam.

Maybe this is what the perch saw
dangling from hooks in the green shallows.
I remember hanging from docks

my bangs fanned in cool water
while I watched them hesitate,
      then move
            unable to resist
to take the mussel and flash silver.

These mussels smell of garlic, onions, something
I don't know, fennel? and
all the grotesque wonderful smells
from childhood – bait and mud and creosote,
diesel and the pulp mill down the bay,
my mother's body hot in the sun
after swimming in salt water.

I catch them on my tongue.

Eight Years Old

All of it, equally
beautiful then

thin layer of indigo
painted under the herring's armor

crusted circles, puckering stars
fish scales dried to my body

how candlefish, swimming,
taper – but that's not why

all rays of light radiate from my head
as I look at the water

tremble, delicate tremble
when my father clubs the rock cod

stomach in mouth, distended, pushing
the furious climb to sunlight

and somehow we grow up
to despise violence

but yearning for simple beauty
to haul us up

and overpower us,
language bursting our throats.

This Is Not

This is not a poem about who I am
or who my father was to me. It carefully
avoids that first memory from a crib,
looking up at his sharp-shooting medals
hung just out of reach, their metallic
refulgence glinting in moonlight.

It makes no mention of the heart
nor of the elk liver carved neatly
into slabs, dredged in flour, and fried
in a pan with bacon and onions. This
is not a poem about any kind of hunger
or the collapse of blood valves in the mouth.

We aren't going out between the islands
tufted with fir and cedar; there is just no way
.to chart where fathers take us, anyway –
even if you think you almost get there
when you dream of breathing underwater.
I don't know about your father. But

I imagine you never thanked him, either,
not really. If he grew old enough to show
how soft he was, how soft he had been
for you all along, what then? You'd made
your glancing peace with hardness,
with sparks that die, sparks that glint.

False Memories

I have one where I'm standing in the doorway of my grandmother's
bedroom and for the first time ever I see her breasts. I see old lady
breasts. I see her standing in front of her mirror getting dressed. I see
her bed with the coverlet she and Papa carefully fold back together
each night, before he goes to sleep in another room. I see the large
oval frame on the wall: her parents, shoulder to shoulder in
Denmark, in black. Until I was ten I thought they were Siamese twins.
That part is true. I see the sheer white curtains stir at each window and
I see my grandmother's breasts. They are so long, so very long.
They hang below her waist, the texture of stretched bread dough.
My grandmother stands in front of her mirror getting dressed.
She picks up her breast and holds it in both hands. She folds the
nipple up into the breast, then folds again, turning the breast over and
over carefully like a cinnamon roll all the way up to her chest, and into
her brassiere, where it belongs. I'll admit I have no memory of what
happens next.

There's another where I'm three and my father opens the screen door
to the kitchen and teases me and I say *I'm not afraid of you!* He says,
You'd better be and strikes with his hand and I fall back, and back, and
down, and down the six concrete steps to the ground. He wouldn't
have really done that. My mother wouldn't have stood in the driveway
with her hand to her waist and told me to go away, she could grow
other babies to take my place. I don't know why my teal green bike is
on its side on the lawn behind her, plastic streamers sprouting from
the handlebars, just like they did in real life.

The gray areas. Photos whose stories I have been told so often it's like
I was there. And sometimes I was: that's me catching chipmunks in a
potato-chip box.

There ought to be a separate place for the false memories, for conve-
nience sake. Just to keep it straight. I'd put some things there. The bear
I could not break eye contact with in the unfinished attic. The night I
reached down between the bed and the wall and my arm came off. The
uncle who made me sit right next to him in his pickup truck, who held
his hand inside my thigh while we drove through the red and gold

woods. We both liked that song on the radio, *Gypsies, Tramps and Thieves*, but I could surrender Cher and Sonny too, with the stolen hours that never really even happened.

Let go of the false memories. Let them all go. Then there would be room, maybe, to recover important things strangely erased. Tasting carrots in the garden, tasting good warm dirt. Walking on strong tanned legs that don't jiggle at all. Why my best friend in elementary school was an Indian boy; what we spoke of for whole summer days fishing from the Guemes Island ferry dock; what the churning white water exposed each time that boat docked and departed.

I could stand to remember one moment in the presence of a man I loved, unaware of the rind of fat riding my hips.

I know the truth is unfolding somewhere, just beyond my consciousness. It's safely hidden in a familiar room where I stand alone and admire myself, redolent of yeast and cinnamon.

One Thing then Another

Wild huckleberry: how the leaves all begin
as pink buds – tiny scrolls of pastel tissue paper
tip the delicate, winter-verdigrised branches,
fragile and spot-lit through forest canopy.
This is not blossoming, no: the green leaf pushes
through, pink tissue opening, a jacket folding back
today as this March world expands into foliage.

And I wonder, would I have ever noticed
the one thing without the other? Washing,
my clitoris, how it works – the sheath:
really seeing something that must have been
living this way all along. And there, beside it,
the smaller lips: how on one side they are
broken, torn apart, and healed ragged.
This Spring a kind of gripping, an almost
knowing what the body tries to say.

Elsa

Winter afternoons she is turtle-like,
hunkered on the blue chair without neck or legs,
an implacable circle of cold fur –
wet dot eyes staring from beneath the desk top.

She is the not dominant housecat,
chased daily, often cornered,
often forced to look back with hard eyes
from beneath the severe M of her tabby forehead –
often waiting for the other one
to have had enough.

And this is her place in the world,
this chair above the baseboard heater.
Without understanding electricity
or how the snow falls outside the window,
piles on Mount Baker, then comes out
beneath the desk as warmth,
she trusts her whole life long
that the heat will come back on.

And then, like a snake in the sun
(or for that matter like the outside cats
who stretch lordly upon the oil-stained pavement
and dare me to run them down),
then she will uncoil with the inhuman grace
of everything that understands its own immortality,
her white-rimmed eyes pressed tight
in ecstasy.

This Road

"A fox, of a kind said to be peculiar to the island,
and very rare in it, was sitting on the rocks. He was
so intently absorbed in watching the surveyors' manoeuvres,
that I was able, by quietly walking up behind, to
knock him on the head with my geological hammer."
—Charles Darwin, *Voyage of the* Beagle

This road goes to my parents' house
(their hawthorn bush, the honey bees
we kept in jam and pickle jars),
and farther back to grandfather's farmhouse,
a bright line of nuisance skunks and foxes
strung by tails from the black walnut tree.
All the way back to that father of us all,
whose address I've forgotten,
but it's a famous old Dominion.

Tonight I'm driving with a summer sunset
in my left eye, each landmark a memory
of some other trip. Just here, the place
we hit a deer (Dad said it must have flown
into a tree because he walked that field
with a flashlight but never found her).
This soft shoulder where we all got out,
to really look at the porcupine's quills.

Tonight the hawks line Highway 20
(except for the two ruffled smears in the road).
Posturing their James Dean shoulders
they clench the human casualty markers.
Mile after mile the crosses appear; here's one
for the man who drank too much once,
one for the soldier (with flowers),
one for the mistake of foolish young people,
and one for the girl who just fell asleep.

Tonight I don't know why we bear
more remembrance than the jagged-faced opossum
whose body breaks beneath our tire.
These crosses signify our difference from them,
the forms that fall and shatter and serve
as their own headstones
until they find some better purpose.

Driving down this road, I anticipate arriving
home to the two cats sitting just inside the door,
their shining eyes upturned to mine.
And I can hardly conceive their tolerance –
how they meet us with their living eyes –
or our arrogance, to look right back.

After Easter

I want to tell you
I am not interested in nature as a metaphor.
Nature is the thing itself
and everything else is metaphor.

I hear the little frogs tonight
singing in the rain, the warm March rain.
You would think those frogs
much bigger than they are.
Their voices sing no metaphors.
The rain is wet and good.

I am trying to understand my friend's
death as metaphor.
Cancer took her, twenty-six weeks pregnant
and knowing the risk of this pregnancy, choosing
it anyway.
The surgeon lifted out a child
the weight of five sticks of butter
more or less
lighter than the weight
of all the metaphors we imagine
she can contain.

Tell me this birth is transcendence.
Or tell me – is this the thing itself?

Yesterday we ate the ham and said the grace but
I want to tell you
I am not interested in resurrection,
and ascension is denial of the thing itself –
denial of my good friend's true
and emptied body in the silent hospital room
with the machines turned off,
denial of the bog just down the road
from us all, the chorus of voices
that stop, and wait, and rise again,
almost like a metaphor, damn it.

Unaccountable
for Gabi

I understand I should not write
of beauty these days
for all the obvious reasons
and my own friend dead these five months now
and I'm not over
not nearly over
any of it.

But I can't help it, am powerless to stop
noticing the bug on my bathroom wall
is a miniature dragonfly,
iridescent blue counties
occupying the paper map of each wing.

Driving to the park-and-ride
I took a deep breath of May morning
and smelled summer coming
and joy
and the remains of Walt Whitman
in the scent of fresh-laid asphalt.

And today I am not afraid of death
because everything in this world is
beauty

even the coal-black asphalt
even the crows that dive and scream
at the confused young hawk soaring too near their nest
at the edge of the trailer park.

Yes, the trailer park too,
its magenta rhododendrons more brilliant than aluminum
its t.v. antennas writing the Chinese character for happiness
fifteen times against the sky.

And me, as I stood unaccountably still
in the graveled park-and-ride lot,

head back, watching a gull breaststroke the universe,
watching the chalky stream it shat
transform into gorgeous sunlit spangles
and did not even think of moving.

I Believe I Could Kneel

I believe I could kneel
in so many quiet places
where the pale sponge of moss
would surely reach above
my hips as I sank down and down
as the deer must in their beds
kneeling once, then once again
to lower themselves front and back
before closing their glistening eyes.

I think I am the kind of person
down on one knee and shifting my weight
my whole life long
but capable of sinking far, and deep,
to the bottom of something
that might replace the religion I discarded
or make me really live in this body
or waste my life.

I would like to live my way into being
someone who stands back up
and runs toward that holy forest.

Mercury

This morning I think about the men I've loved
so differently, about the one's salty hands
and another who held his tongue
to the edge of his own lips at every moment
of concentration. And the one with all the cats,
who appeared only to love cats and nobody
else. And I think about the cats I've loved
so differently. The blue Russian who jumped
from a sidewalk into my arms the first time we met.
The Siamese who suckled any soft bit of me
he could draw into his hot pink mouth.
And this one – with loose and gorgeous belly
all flab and sunshine watching me now,
watching me try the same poem again and again:
thinking each time *I am writing something new*
the way we think each love is new
when really it's the same love again and again
squirting sideways between our fingers, rolling over
a tabletop, beads of mercury breaking and rejoining,
traveling the floorboards to settle and tremble
and wait in the cracks. There is no end to the matter
of love, no dissolution – and this is the poem
I'll write again tomorrow. Although you may read it
so differently, I think we all bear the same message
of enduring   changing   love

A Note About the Cover

Sarni Pootoogook, "Blue Bird and Sedna" (2002)
Etching and aquatint
Permission for use granted by Dorset Fine Arts

Sarni Pootoogook (1922–2003) was a member of a well-known family of Inuit artists. She participated in the early years of the printmaking program in Canada's Cape Dorset (Baffin Island) – a program that in 1959 introduced Western materials to traditional Inuit of her generation, producing a new and stunning form of art. After taking a long hiatus from her work as a graphic artist, to care for her family, she returned to printmaking and the Cape Dorset graphic arts community late in life. Her images are known for their style combining boldness and whimsy.

Sedna appears frequently in Inuit sculpture and prints. She is a powerful spirit at home in the sea, having the head and torso of a woman and the tail of a fish. The legend of how the creatures of the sea came to exist, and how Sedna (known as Talelaya in the Inuktutut language) became the deity who provides animals for the Inuit, is told in many different ways throughout the Arctic.

In one legend, Sedna was a child with a tremendous appetite – so hungry was she that she tried to devour her father's arm as he slept. When he awoke, her father took Sedna on the sea and threw her overboard. She clung to the side of the boat until her father chopped off her fingers. As each finger fell into the water, it was transformed into a different animal – the seals, whales, walrus, and sea lions.

In another Sedna creation story, this child lived in contentment with her father and mother and refused to marry until her parents insisted. A bird disguised as a handsome man visited her and promised she would live in luxury and have plenty to eat if she married him. She did, and he took her away to his island – where she discovered he was just a bird who could only provide fish to eat and a hovel to inhabit. When Sedna's father came to visit, he killed the bird and attempted to take Sedna home across the water. But all the other birds flapped their wings and created a storm. Sedna's father grew afraid and threw her overboard to appease the birds. In this story too, Sedna's father cut off each of her fingers, and they transformed into the animals of the sea.

When a traditional Inuit hunter is given a seal, he drops water into its mouth in a gesture of gratitude to Sedna. If the hunters of a community are unlucky for a long time, the shaman will transform herself or himself into a fish and will swim to the bottom of the sea to Sedna. The shaman combs the tangles from Sedna's hair and braids it. Perhaps because Sedna has lost her fingers, she cannot do this for herself. Calmed, Sedna allows her animals to give themselves to the Inuit again.

Design and Production

Text and cover design by Kathy Boykowycz

Text set in ITC Giovanni, designed in 1989 by Robert Slimbach
Titles set in Frutiger, designed in 1975 by Adrian Frutiger

Printed by Thomson-Shore of Dexter, Michigan,
on Nature's Natural, a 50% recycled paper